Writer's Notebook

GRADE 1

Contents

MODULE 1: Oral Story

MODULE 2: Descriptive Essay

MODULE 3: Informational Text

MODULE 4: Informational Text

MODULE 5: Imaginative Story

MODULE 6: Personal Narrative

MODULE 7: Poem

MODULE 8: Personal Narrative

MODULE 9: Informational Text

MODULE 10: Informational Text

MODULE 11: Opinion Letter

MODULE 12: Opinion Essay

Name _____

Words About Writing

Draw pictures and label them in each box.

People	Animals
_____ - - - - - - - - - - - - _____	_____ - - - - - - - - - - - - _____
Places	**Things**
_____ - - - - - - - - - - - - _____	_____ - - - - - - - - - - - - _____

Name _____

My Goals

In this module, you will tell an oral story about something that has happened to you.

Have you ever told a story to someone? What did you do well? What do you want to do better? Read these goals carefully and write #1 next to the one you most want to work on.

I will...

☐	Brainstorm my ideas, listing many possible topics.
☐	Choose a story to tell that will be interesting for others to hear.
☐	Organize my story into steps.
☐	Include important details.
☐	Practice good speaking skills when I tell my story.
☐	Practice good listening skills when others are telling their stories.

Brainstorming

Write and draw about an event.

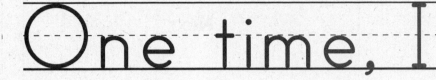

One time, I

Name _____

My Story Grid

Draw and label the events in order.

First	Next
Then	**Last**

1.4

Name _____

Class Story Grid

Draw and label the events in order.

First	Next
Then	**Last**

Draft Class Story

Write the events in order.

First, _____

_____

Next, _____

_____

Then, _____

_____

Last, _____

_____

Find the Proper Nouns

Circle the proper nouns. There are one or more proper nouns in each sentence.

1. My friend Susie lives on Main Street.

2. Susie and I have been friends for a long time.

3. We were both in Mr. Hill's kindergarten class.

4. My dog is named Billy and hers is named Max.

Publish Class Story

Print the class story neatly. Use your best handwriting.
Be sure to leave a finger space between words and
after end punctuation.

Title: _____

_____

_____

_____

_____

_____

_____

Develop Imagery

What things did the song make you imagine? Draw the pictures you saw in your head as you listened to the song.

Name _____

Word Bank

Listen as your teacher reads the focal text again. Listen for words that are unfamiliar or that create images in your mind. Write the words and draw pictures of them below.

Name _____

My Wonderful World

What makes where you live a wonderful place? Draw pictures and add words to show some specific things that make your world wonderful.

Name _____

My Goals

In this module, you will write an informational text explaining what makes your world wonderful.

Think about your past writing. What did you do well? What do you want to do better? Read these goals carefully and write #1 next to the one you most want to improve.

I will...

☐	Choose to write about something that I want to share with my friends.
☐	Explain why what I chose makes my world wonderful.
☐	Use new words that appeal to the five senses.
☐	Draw pictures to help show what I am explaining.
☐	Use the new writing process I have learned.
☐	Use new capitalization skills I have learned.

Name _____

My Wonderful World

Draw a picture and write about what makes your world wonderful.

_____

- -

_____

_____

- -

_____

_____

- -

_____

_____

- -

_____

Name _____

Writer's Model

My Wonderful World

I ride my bicycle in the park. I smell the fresh air.

Name _____

I see the purple flowers. I love their sweet smell.

Name _____

I love to climb trees.
I see their green
leaves.

Common and Proper Nouns

For each common noun, write a proper noun that names a specific person, place, or thing.

Common Noun	Proper Noun
street	Main Street
lake	
teacher	
friend	
town	
book	

Name _____

Editing Checklist

Ask these questions as you edit your pages.

Does the writing explain what makes their world wonderful?	YES NO
Does the writing include sensory details?	YES NO
Are there pictures that help the explanation?	YES NO
Are proper nouns capitalized?	YES NO
Does the writing use proper line spacing?	YES NO

Final Touches

Find one sentence in your writing that you think could be better. Write that sentence on the lines below.

_____
- -
_____
- -
_____
- -
_____

Work with a partner to rewrite your sentence. What can you change to make it easier to understand? Write your new sentence on the lines below. Use your best handwriting. Leave spaces between words.

_____
- -
_____
- -
_____
- -
_____
- -

Find the Feature

With your group, search through a copy of <u>Giraffes</u>, looking for each of the following items. As you find each one, write the page number (or numbers) in the box next to it.

Table of Contents . . . . page ⬚

Words to Know . . . . page ⬚

Picture a Giraffe. . . . . page ⬚

Read More. . . . . page ⬚

Index . . . . page ⬚

Word Bank

Listen to <u>Giraffes</u>. Write down interesting words you hear.

My Amazing Animals

Write or draw any animals you would like to learn more about.

Name _____

My Goals

In this module, you will write an all-about book about your favorite animal.

Think about your past writing. What did you do well? What do you want to do better? Read these goals carefully and write #1 next to the one you most want to improve.

I will...

☐	Choose a topic that readers want to know more about.
☐	Explain why I chose that topic.
☐	Include interesting and relevant facts about my topic.
☐	Draw pictures to support my writing.
☐	Use new grammar skills I have learned.
☐	Use new capitalization and punctuation skills I have learned.

Finding Facts

Write some facts about your animal in the spaces below.

> Where My Animal Lives

> What My Animal Eats

> Interesting Facts About My Animal

Name _____

My All-About Book

Use your research from Writer's Notebook page 3.5 to write about your animal.

_____

- -

_____

- -

_____

- -

_____

- -

_____

- -

_____

- -

_____

- -

_____

- -

_____

Writer's Model

All About Horses

Table of Contents

My Favorite Animal

Horses are my favorite animal. They are smart and do many jobs for humans.

1

Where Horses Live

Today, most horses live on farms and ranches. Some horses, like police horses, live in big cities.

2

What Horses Eat

Horses eat grass and hay. They also like oats and corn. Many horses also like carrots and apples.

3

Table of Contents

Look back over your research essay and page numbers. Write out your table of contents with the page numbers below.

_____
- · · · · · · page [   ]
_____

_____
- · · · · · · page [   ]
_____

_____
- · · · · · · page [   ]
_____

_____
- · · · · · · page [   ]
_____

_____
- · · · · · · page [   ]
_____

Name _____

Editing Checklist

Ask these questions as you edit your page.

Do sentences begin with capital letters?	YES	NO
Do sentences end with punctuation?	YES	NO
Are the singular and plural nouns correct?	YES	NO
Does it say where the animal lives?	YES	NO
Does it say what the animal eats?	YES	NO
Does it have pictures of the animal?	YES	NO
Do the pictures match the text?	YES	NO

Name _____

Animal Facts

What fun facts have you learned about your animal? Write your answers neatly below. Be sure to use your best handwriting. Leave spaces between your words and sentences.

Word Bank

Listen to <u>Do Unto Otters</u>. Write interesting words in the chart. Add definitions for the words.

Word	Definition

Name _____

Brainstorming

Brainstorm ways to make friends. Then add an illustration.

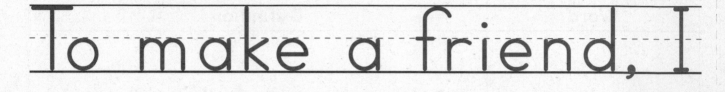

To make a friend, I

Graphic Organizer

Think about one way to make a new friend. Make drawings of the steps. Be sure to draw the steps in the order they should be done.

Step 1

Step 2

Step 3

Step 4

Name _____

My Goals

In this module, you will write a how-to text about making a friend.

Think about your past writing. What did you do well? What do you want to do better? Read these goals carefully and write #1 next to the one you most want to improve.

I will...

☐	Write a clear beginning sentence that introduces my topic.
☐	Write a strong ending sentence that wraps up the how-to text.
☐	Write my steps in order.
☐	Start each sentence with a capital letter.
☐	End each sentence with punctuation.

How to Make a Friend

- Circle the introduction.

- Draw a box around the body.

- Draw two lines under the conclusion.

I love making new friends.

1. I see someone sitting alone.

2. I walk up to her.

3. I smile and say, "Hi."

4. I invite her to play a game with me.

Making new friends is fun.

Name _____

How to Make a Friend

Use one page for each step of your how-to text. First, write the words for each part of the how-to text. Then, add the illustrations.

_____
- - - - - - - - - - - - - - - - - -
_____

_____
- - - - - - - - - - - - - - - - - -
_____

_____
- - - - - - - - - - - - - - - - - -
_____

_____
- - - - - - - - - - - - - - - - - -
_____

Name _____

Writer's Model

How to Make a Friend

First, I see someone sitting alone.

Name _____

Then, I walk up to her.

Next, I smile and say,
"Hi."

Name _____

Last, I invite her to play a game with me. Making new friends is fun.

Name _____

Group Sharing

Listen to others share their how-to texts. Take notes to help you remember. Share your notes with the writer.

- Was the beginning/introduction clear and interesting?

- After hearing the beginning, am I sure what the writing is about?

- Are the steps in order?

- Do the steps make sense?

- Are the words carefully chosen and clear?

- Does the ending/conclusion wrap things up?

Name _____

Make It Clearer

Can you find a sentence in your writing that you think could be better? Copy the sentence neatly on the lines below. Be sure to leave spaces between words.

_____

- - - - - - - - - - - - - - - - - - - -

_____

_____

Work with a partner to rewrite your sentence and make it easier to understand. Write your new sentence on the lines below.

_____

- - - - - - - - - - - - - - - - - - - -

_____

- - - - - - - - - - - - - - - - - - - -

_____

Name _____

Singular and Plural Nouns

Work with a partner to create a list of singular and plural nouns from <u>Do Unto Otters</u>.

Singular Nouns	Plural Nouns

Editing Checklist

Ask these questions as you edit your how-to text.

Do sentences begin with capital letters?	YES	NO
Does the text include time-order words?	YES	NO
Are the steps in correct order?	YES	NO
Are the words spelled correctly?	YES	NO
Do sentences end with punctuation?	YES	NO

Name _____

Things That Come and Go

Make a list of things in nature that come and go.

_____

- -

_____

- -

_____

- -

_____

- -

_____

- -

_____

- -

_____

- -

_____

- -

_____

- -

_____

I Wonder Why

Make a list of things in nature that you wonder about.

_____

- - - - - - - - - - - - - - - - - - - -

_____

- - - - - - - - - - - - - - - - - - - -

_____

- - - - - - - - - - - - - - - - - - - -

_____

- - - - - - - - - - - - - - - - - - - -

_____

- - - - - - - - - - - - - - - - - - - -

_____

- - - - - - - - - - - - - - - - - - - -

_____

- - - - - - - - - - - - - - - - - - - -

_____

Word Bank

Listen to <u>Why the Sun and the Moon Live in the Sky</u>. Write down interesting time and place words you hear.

Name _____

Summarize the Folktale

Write down and illustrate three ideas that summarize <u>Why the Sun and the Moon Live in the Sky</u>.

Idea 1	Idea 2	Idea 3

Folktale Words

Write down some words you've heard in different folktales that describe beginnings, endings, and settings.

_____

- -

_____

- -

_____

- -

_____

- -

_____

- -

_____

- -

_____

- -

_____

Name _____

My Goals

In this module, you will write a folktale about how something in nature came to be.

Think about your past writing. What did you do well? What do you want to do better? Read these goals carefully and write #1 next to the one you most want to improve.

I will...

☐	Include a sentence to introduce my characters.
☐	Describe the setting.
☐	Use action words to describe the beginning, middle, and ending.
☐	Include a problem and a solution.
☐	Use nouns and pronouns.
☐	Use new capitalization and punctuation skills I have learned.

Name _____

Brainstorm an Idea

Brainstorm an idea for your folktale. Ask **who**, **what**, **where**, **when**, and **why** questions. Draw pictures that help illustrate your ideas.

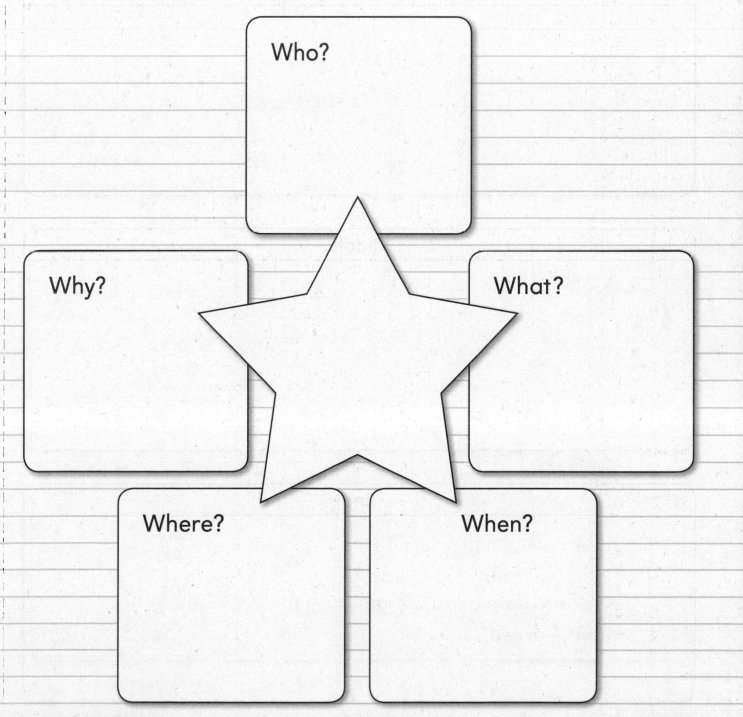

Name _____

Beginning, Middle, End

Your folktale should include a beginning, a middle, and an end.

Beginning

Middle

End

Name _____

Problem and Solution

Your folktale should include a problem and a solution.

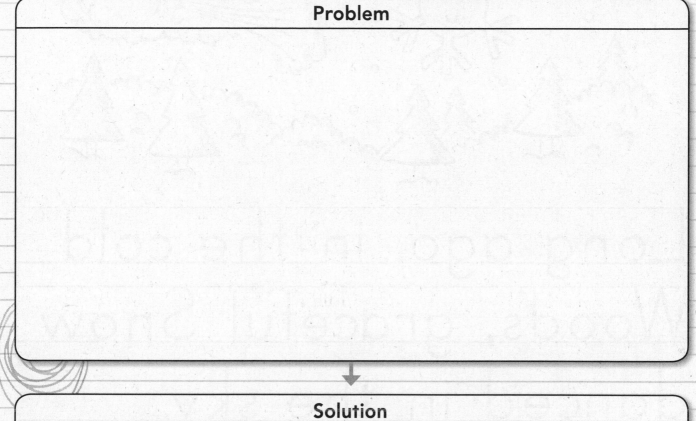

Problem

Solution

Name _____

Writer's Model

Long ago, in the cold Woods, graceful Snow danced in the sky. Snow loved to gather flakes. Snow was happy when Cold Wind blew.

One day, warm air flooded the sky. Cold Wind shook. "It is my cousin, Warm Wind!" Warm Wind said, "Leave, Cold Wind! It is my turn to blow."

Snow said, "It is time for a new dance. Warm Wind should blow. I will go away. But I will return for you again in winter, Cold Wind!"

5.12

Pronouns Word Bank

You can use pronouns to replace other nouns and create variety in your writing. Add different pronouns below.

Verbs That Tell Time

Read the sentences below and circle the past-tense verbs.

1. Sun and Moon invited Water to visit.

2. Water replied, "My family is very big."

3. Moon greeted Water with a smile.

4. Sun and Moon lived in a house.

5. Then they lived in the sky.

Name _____

Editing Checklist

Ask these questions as you edit your folktale.

Do sentences begin with capital letters?	YES	NO
Do sentences end with punctuation?	YES	NO
Does the folktale include a variety of verbs?	YES	NO
Does the folktale have a beginning, a middle, and an end?	YES	NO
Does the story have elements of a folktale?	YES	NO
Does the folktale use pronouns?	YES	NO

Name _____

Word Bank

Listen as your teacher reads <u>The Thanksgiving Door</u> again. Listen for words that are unfamiliar or that create images in your mind. Write the words and draw pictures of them below.

Name _____

Your Favorite Holiday

Think about your favorite holiday. Ask **who**, **what**, **when**, **where**, and **how** questions.

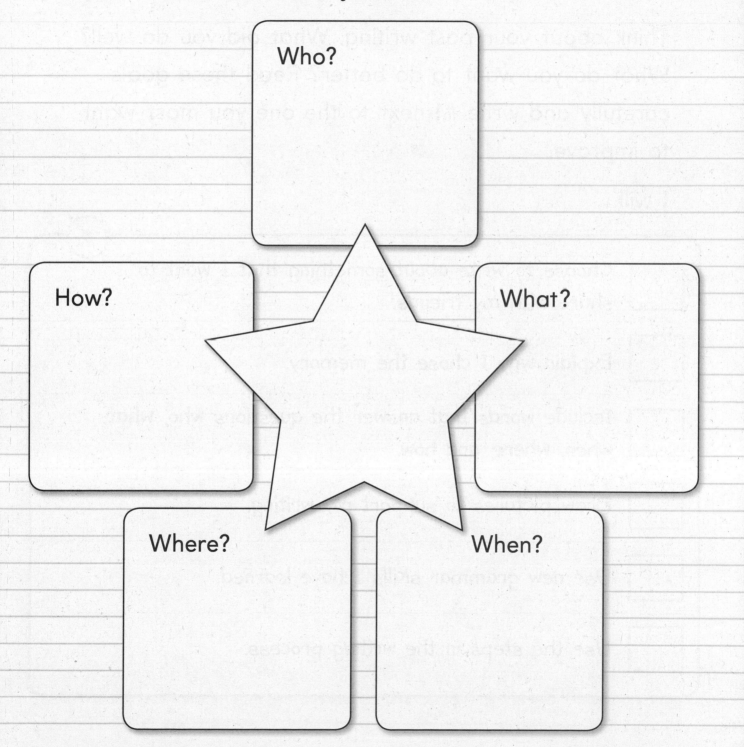

Name _____

My Goals

In this module, you will write a personal narrative about a favorite holiday memory.

Think about your past writing. What did you do well? What do you want to do better? Read these goals carefully and write #1 next to the one you most want to improve.

I will...

☐	Choose to write about something that I want to share with my friends.
☐	Explain why I chose the memory.
☐	Include words that answer the questions **who**, **what**, **when**, **where**, and **how**.
☐	Draw pictures to support my writing.
☐	Use new grammar skills I have learned.
☐	Use the steps in the writing process.

Name _____

Planning Chart

List what happens at the beginning, middle, and end of your story.

Beginning	Middle	End

Name _____

My Favorite Holiday Memory

Draft your personal narrative. Include a beginning, a middle, and an end. Illustrate your draft.

Writer's Model

July Fourth
Block Party

On July Fourth, we
had a block party on
our street. My family
and neighbors were
there. It was a blast.

My neighbor hung up
a piñata. We all tried
to hit it, but it
wouldn't break! Then
I had an idea.

Name _____

Mom took down the piñata. Dad got his bowling ball. He dropped it. The piñata broke open! I smiled.

Name _____

Three Questions

Answer the questions. Print neatly. Leave spaces between words.

1. What happens at the beginning?

_____

- -

_____

- -

_____

2. What happens in the middle?

_____

- -

_____

- -

_____

3. What happens at the end?

_____

- -

_____

- -

_____

My Complete Sentence

Write a complete sentence about a picture. Print neatly. Leave spaces between words.

Name _____

Editing Checklist

Ask these questions as you edit your story.

Does each *sentence* have a *subject*?	YES	NO
Does each *sentence* have a *verb*?	YES	NO
Does each *sentence* *begin* with a capital letter?	YES	NO
Does each *sentence* end with punctuation?	YES	NO

Name _____

Class Poem

Write a copy of the class poem below. Use your best handwriting and leave spaces between words and sentences.

_____
- -
_____

_____
- -
_____

_____
- -
_____

_____
- -
_____

_____
- -
_____

_____
- -
_____

Word Bank

Listen to <u>Ask Me</u>. Write down interesting nature and action words you hear.

Name _____

Poetry Challenge

Write the short poem your group created below. Print
neatly, with finger spaces between the words and
after the end punctuation of the sentences.

My Topics

Think of a few things you like in nature. Write them in the boxes.

Name _____

My Goals

In this module, you will write a poem about things you like in nature.

Think about your past writing. What did you do well? What do you want to do better? Read these goals carefully and write #1 next to the one you most want to improve.

I will...

- [ ] Choose an interesting topic about nature.
- [ ] Write in free verse or use rhyme.
- [ ] Use nature nouns and action verbs.
- [ ] Use onomatopoeia or rhythm.
- [ ] Use correct spelling, capitalization, and punctuation.

Poem Planning Chart

Think about your poem topic. Then write words that describe the feelings, senses, and actions of your topic in the chart.

Feelings	Senses	Actions

Writer's Model

Butterflies

Flutter in the wind
Float in the sky,
Quiet dance
Catch my eye.

Orange and brown,
Yellow and black,
Find a flower,
Eat a snack!

Butterflies

Butterflies

Orange, yellow

Fluttering, flittering, fleeting

Jewels of the fall

Monarchs

Name _____

How to Write a Cinquain

When you read or write a cinquain, each word has a very special meaning. This type of poem gets its shape and its organization from the set of rules below. Use these rules to read the model poem on page 7.8. Afterward, you can try writing your own cinquain! The way words appear in a cinquain is very important, so write neatly with careful spaces between words.

Line 1: one noun that is the topic of the poem

Line 2: two adjectives describing the topic

Line 3: three words that end in –**ing** that describe an action made by the topic

Line 4: a four-word phrase that expresses a feeling about the topic

Line 5: a word that means the same thing as the topic

Adding Sound

Brainstorm words that create rhythm that you can use in your poem.

Rhyme	
Repeating Words	
Same Letter Sounds	
Onomatopoeia	

Name _____

Listening Checklist

Ask these questions as you revise your poem.

Are there nature words?	YES	NO
Are there sound words?	YES	NO
Does the poem have a rhythm?	YES	NO
Are there "sense" words?	YES	NO
Does the poem rhyme?	YES	NO

Which Verb Agrees?

Circle the verb that agrees with the subject in each of these sentences.

1. The boom of thunder (make/makes) me jump.

2. The meows of my cat (tell/tells) me she is hungry.

3. The car horns (toot/toots).

4. The cow (moo/moos).

5. The jumping frog (plop/plops) into the pond.

Editing Checklist

Ask these questions as you edit your poem.

Do sentences begin with capital letters?	YES	NO
Do sentences end with punctuation?	YES	NO
Does the poem use line breaks?	YES	NO
Are words spelled correctly?	YES	NO
Do all subjects and verbs agree?	YES	NO

Word Bank

Listen to <u>The Kissing Hand</u>. Write down interesting words you hear.

Name _____

My Topics

Think of a few problems you have faced and how someone helped you solve them. Write the problem and solution pairs in the chart.

Problem	Solution

Name _____

My Goals

In this module, you will write a personal narrative about someone who helped you solve a problem. This story is about your real life.

Think about your past writing. What did you do well? What do you want to do better? Read these goals carefully and write #1 next to the one you most want to improve.

I will...

☐	Choose a story idea that readers will want to read.
☐	Write the beginning, middle, and end of the story.
☐	Use new words I have learned.
☐	Draw pictures to show what is happening in my story.
☐	Use new grammar skills I have learned.
☐	Use new capitalization and punctuation skills I have learned.

Star Organizer

Write the title of your story in the star. Then complete the organizer with your story ideas.

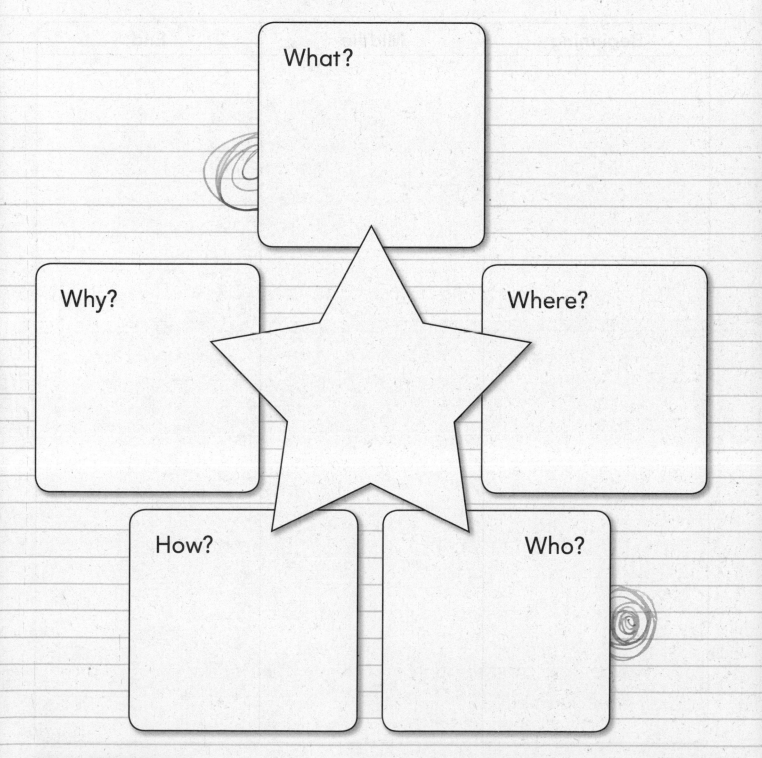

What?

Why?

Where?

How?

Who?

My Story Outline

Use your Star Organizer to help you write a beginning, middle, and end in the chart.

Beginning	Middle	End

Name _____

Different Endings

Write a surprise ending, happy ending, and a lesson ending to your story.

Type of Ending	My Example
1. Surprise Ending	
2. Happy Ending	
3. Lesson Ending	

Name _____

Writer's Model

Where's Jack?
One day, my friend
and I went outside to
play with my dog
Jack. We looked in the
yard. He was gone!

8.7

"Oh no! Jack's lost!"
I cried.
My friend said, "I'll
help you find him!" We
searched everywhere.

Name _____

Suddenly, we heard a crunching noise from a leaf pile. Out popped Jack! I was so happy to see him!

Adding Adjectives

When you add adjectives to a sentence, you give your reader a more detailed picture of your ideas. Add adjectives to the following sentences.

_____

1. My favorite blanket is _____

_____

and _____ .

_____

2. Everyone enjoyed the _____ book the teacher read to us.

_____

3. The _____ knight fought the

_____

_____ dragon.

_____

4. The _____ butterfly landed on the

_____

_____ flower.

Name _____

Clocking Checklist

Check for these items as you edit.

Includes a problem and solution.	YES	NO
Has a beginning, middle, and end.	YES	NO
Uses the pronoun I.	YES	NO
Uses vivid words.	YES	NO
Uses dialogue.	YES	NO
The pictures help tell the story.	YES	NO
Uses capital letters.	YES	NO
Uses end punctuation.	YES	NO
The words are spelled correctly.	YES	NO

Word Bank

Listen to <u>One Bean</u>. Write interesting words and new words in the chart below. Use the illustrations and sentence clues.

Word	What It Means

Experiment 1

You will need:

- 1 empty 16-ounce water bottle

- 8–9 inch balloon, which has been stretched out

- small funnel

- ½ cup white vinegar

- 1 teaspoon baking soda

Directions

1. Using the funnel, pour the baking soda into the balloon.

2. Pour the white vinegar into the empty bottle.

3. Carefully stretch the balloon over the neck of the bottle.

4. Lift the balloon and let the baking soda drop into the vinegar.

5. Watch what happens next!

Experiment 1: What Happened?

Write and draw your answers to the questions below.

What did you see during the experiment?

What do you think happened?

Experiment 2

You will need:

- 1 raw egg

- 1 hard-boiled egg

- 2 plates

- 1 marker

Directions

1. Using the marker, write the number 1 on the raw egg. Put the egg on a plate.

2. Write the number 2 on the hard-boiled egg. Put the egg on the other plate.

3. Spin the eggs on their sides or on their ends. Try lots of different spins!

4. How are the spins of the two eggs different?

Experiment 2: What Happened?

Write and draw your answers to the questions below.

What did you see?

What do you think happened?

Name _____

My Goals

In this module, you will write a descriptive essay about a science experiment.

Think about your past writing. What did you do well? What do you want to do better? Read these goals carefully and write #1 next to the one you most want to improve.

I will...

☐	Write a clear *beginning* sentence.
☐	Use descriptive words.
☐	Use transition words to help my essay flow.
☐	Use different types of sentences.
☐	Start each sentence with a capital letter.
☐	End each sentence with correct punctuation.
☐	Write a strong *ending* sentence.

Descriptive Essay Web

Write your topic in the center box. Use your notes on Writer's Notebook page 9.3 or 9.5 to fill in the other boxes.

Name _____

Flowers Change Color! Draft

- Circle the introduction.

- Draw a box around the body.

- Draw two lines under the conclusion.

Flowers can change color.

We filled a glass with water.

We added food coloring to the water.

We put a white flower in the water.

Water went up the stem.

The white flower turned blue.

My Science Experiment Essay

Look at your web on Writer's Notebook page 9.7.
Draft your descriptive essay on the lines below.
Illustrate your draft.

Writer's Model

Flowers Change Color!

Did you know flowers can change color? We did an experiment. First, we filled a tall glass with cold water.

Then, we added blue food coloring to the water. Next, we put a white flower in the blue water. Later, we observed that the flower was blue!

Name _____

What happened? We discovered that the blue water went up the stem. It turned the white petals blue. It was amazing!

Name _____

Descriptive Words

Circle descriptive words in the sentences.
Illustrate each sentence.

1. Soon two leaves grew on my bean plant.

2. My little plant was too big for its plastic pot.

3. The bean plant grew many white flowers with soft petals.

4. I moved my pretty plant to a sunny kitchen window.

Group Sharing

Listen to the author. Take notes. Share your thoughts.

Does the introduction get your attention?

Does it have descriptive words? Relevant details?
Transition words?

Are the steps in order?

Does the conclusion retell the main idea?

Name _____

Types of Sentences

Read the sentence. Add end punctuation. Decide what kind of sentence it is.

Highlight declarative sentences **yellow**.

Highlight interrogative sentences **green**.

Highlight imperative sentences **pink**.

Highlight exclamatory sentences **blue**.

1. Do you like science_____

2. I like doing experiments_____

3. Don't spill the water_____

4. I can't wait to see what happens_____

5. Write down what you observed_____

6. The water traveled up the stem_____

7. What color did the flower turn_____

8. I was so surprised_____

Clocking Checklist

Listen to your teacher. Read the essay. Check for the item. Circle **YES** or **NO**. Tell the author one thing you liked about the essay.

The author used different types of sentences.	**YES NO**
The author used capital letters correctly.	**YES NO**
The author used correct end punctuation.	**YES NO**
The author spelled words correctly.	**YES NO**

My Dreams

Draw some of the things you would like to do in your life.

Name _____

Word Bank

As you read the book <u>The Girl Who Could Dance in</u> <u>Outer Space</u>, write down any interesting and unfamiliar words you find. Use a dictionary, context clues, or illustrations to figure out what the words mean.

10.2

Who Inspires Me?

Draw or list the names of some people who inspire you. As you do this brainstorming activity, ask yourself why you are inspired by them.

My Goals

In this module, you will write a short biography of someone who inspires you.

Think about your past writing. What did you do well? What did you want to do better? Read these goals carefully and write #1 next to the one you most want to improve.

I will...

☐	Tell interesting facts about an inspirational person.
☐	Tell what the person did that inspired me.
☐	Use time-order words to help show when things happened.
☐	Use interesting and vivid words.
☐	Use pronouns correctly.

Research Cards

Use your sources to find out information about the person you chose who inspires you. Fill out the information on the cards below.

When and where was the person born?

What did the person do that was inspiring?

How does this person inspire you?

The Biography of _____

Keep track of the sources you used to do your research by recording the titles, authors, and websites.

Books I Used	
Title	**Author**
Online Sources	

Websites:

Name _____

Writer's Model

Helen Keller

Helen Keller was born
in 1880 in Alabama.
When she was a baby,
she got sick. She
became deaf and
blind.

Because Helen couldn't see or hear, she struggled to learn. Her teacher, Annie Sullivan, taught her sign language.

Name _____

Helen first learned to speak and then to write. She always tried, even when it was hard. She inspires me to never give up!

Name _____

Biography

Draw a picture of the person who inspires you.
Then write their biography below.

_____
- -
_____
- -
_____
- -
_____
- -
_____

Name _____

Pick a Pronoun!

Circle the right pronoun to replace the underlined noun in each sentence.

1. That book is <u>Ella's</u>.   hers   her

2. <u>Marty</u> told a story.   Him   He

3. The joke was told by <u>Scott</u>.   his   him

4. <u>Puja</u> wrote her paper today.   Her   She

5. <u>Maya and Talitha</u> sang a song.   They   Them

Editing Checklist

Ask these questions as you edit your biographical essay.

Does the essay tell about an inspiring person?	YES NO
Does the essay give relevant facts about him or her?	YES NO
Do "time words" help tell the story in order?	YES NO
Does the essay use vivid verbs?	YES NO
Do sentences begin with capital letters?	YES NO
Do sentences end with the right punctuation?	YES NO

Name _____

How, When, Why?

With your classmates, talk about possible answers to these questions:

- How can reading be fun?

- When is reading fun to do?

- Why is reading fun for you?

Then, draw a picture of yourself reading below.

Name _____

Word Bank

Listen as your teacher reads the focal text again. Listen for words that are unfamiliar or that create images in your mind. Write the words and draw pictures of them below.

Name _____

My Favorite Books

Write a list of your favorite books below.

_____

1. _____

_____

2. _____

_____

3. _____

_____

Name _____

My Goals

In this module, you will write an opinion letter about a favorite book.

Think about your past writing. What did you do well? What do you want to do better? Read these goals carefully and write #1 next to the one you most want to improve.

I will...

☐	List everything I know about the person I'm writing to.
☐	Think about the *books* I like and what makes them good.
☐	Choose the right *book* for the person I'm writing to.
☐	Use the new letter writing format I have learned.
☐	Use correct grammar and punctuation.

Name _____

The Boy in the Book

Write down everything you know about the boy in the book. Understanding the boy will help you pick the right book for him.

The boy in the book is...

_____

- -

_____

- -

_____

- -

_____

- -

_____

- -

_____

- -

_____

- -

_____

Name _____

Writer's Model

April 26, 2020

Dear Josh,

I think you should read the book Ralph Tells a Story. You will like it because Ralph is a lot like you. Both you and Ralph have trouble thinking of stories to tell in class.

Ralph learns he has a lot of stories to tell. Reading about him will help you find your stories. Also, you will learn that stories are everywhere.

Sincerely,
Sophia

Name _____

Opinion Letter

Write a draft of your opinion letter to the boy in the book on the lines below.

_____

- -

_____

- -

_____

- -

_____

- -

_____

- -

_____

- -

_____

- -

_____

- -

_____

- -

_____

Name _____

Thank-You Letter

Write a thank-you letter below. Use your best
handwriting. Print each sentence neatly, leaving
a finger space between words.

Date: _____

Dear _____,

Thank you for _____

_____

_____

Yours truly,

_____

Feedback

Use the space below to draw pictures and take notes while your classmates read their opinion letters. Remember to listen for an opinion statement and supporting details.

_____'s Opinion Letter

Opinion Statement:

Supporting Details:

Name _____

Which Verb?

Circle the right verb.

1. The girl (choose   chooses) a book.

2. She (read   reads) about animals.

3. The books (teach   teaches) her many things.

4. Penguins (swim   swims) in cold water.

5. An owl (sleep   sleeps) during the day.

Editing Checklist

Ask these questions as you edit your opinion letter.

Do sentences begin with capital letters?	**YES NO**
Do sentences end with punctuation?	**YES NO**
Do subjects and verbs agree?	**YES NO**
Are words spelled correctly?	**YES NO**
Are dates formatted correctly?	**YES NO**
Are adverbs and prepositions used correctly?	**YES NO**

Word Bank

Listen to <u>Big Bad Bubble</u>. Write down any feeling or opinion words you hear.

Name _____

My Topic

Think of a few skills you have learned in school this year. In one column, make a list of the skills you use the most. In the second column, make a list of the skills you liked learning best. It's okay to put the same skill in both columns.

Skills I Use the Most	Skills I Liked Learning

Name _____

My Goals

In this module, you will write an opinion essay about the best thing you learned how to do in the first grade.

Think about your past writing. What did you do well? What do you want to do better? Read these goals carefully and write #1 next to the one you most want to improve.

I will...

☐	Choose an interesting topic.
☐	Provide reasons for my opinion.
☐	Use proper subject-verb agreement.
☐	Tell how I will use my skill next year.
☐	Use correct spelling, capitalization, and punctuation.

Opinion Planning Map

Complete this map using the topic you chose for your opinion essay.

My Opinion

⬇

Reason 1

⬇

Reason 2

⬇

How I Will Use the Skill Next Year

Name _____

Writer's Model

The Best Skill

The best skill I learned this year was how to be a better listener. It is an important and fun skill to learn.

One reason why listening is the best skill is that it helps me pay attention and learn more in class.

Another reason is that I've made a lot of friends by being a good listener.

I believe this skill will help me learn more and make new friends next year.

Listening is the most helpful skill you can learn to be successful as a student and a friend!

Name _____

My Best Skill

Write your opinion essay on the lines below. Include two reasons for your opinion.

_____

- -

_____

- -

_____

- -

_____

- -

_____

- -

_____

- -

_____

- -

_____

- -

_____

Adding Details

Write down three reasons why you know which skill is the best to learn. Add the reasons you think are most important to your draft.

_____
- - - - - - - - - - - - - - - - - - - -

1. _____

_____
- - - - - - - - - - - - - - - - - - - -

_____

2. _____

_____
- - - - - - - - - - - - - - - - - - - -

_____

3. _____

_____
- - - - - - - - - - - - - - - - - - - -

_____

Conference Checklist

As you listen to your classmates' opinion essays, think about these questions.

- ☐ Does the essay tell the writer's opinion clearly?

- ☐ Does the essay give relevant details that explain the writer's opinion?

- ☐ Does the essay have a conclusion that retells the writer's opinion?

List the feedback your classmates gave you about your opinion essay.

_____

- -

_____

- -

_____

- -

_____

- -

_____

Adverbs That Tell Time

Adverbs help you tell whether something happened in the past, present, or future. Make a list of adverbs that you can use in revising your opinion essay.

Past	Present	Future

Prepositions

Prepositions help link nouns, pronouns, or phrases in a sentence.

Circle the prepositions in each sentence.

1. Her birthday is on November 1.

2. Where will you be on Thanksgiving?

3. I went to my grandma's house in June.

4. School starts at 8:00 a.m.

5. Let's play at lunchtime.

6. Flowers grow in the spring.

Editing Checklist

Ask these questions as you edit your opinion essay.

Do sentences begin with capital letters?	**YES NO**
Do sentences end with punctuation?	**YES NO**
Do subjects and verbs agree?	**YES NO**
Are words spelled correctly?	**YES NO**
Are adverbs and prepositions used correctly?	**YES NO**